My New School

by John Serrano

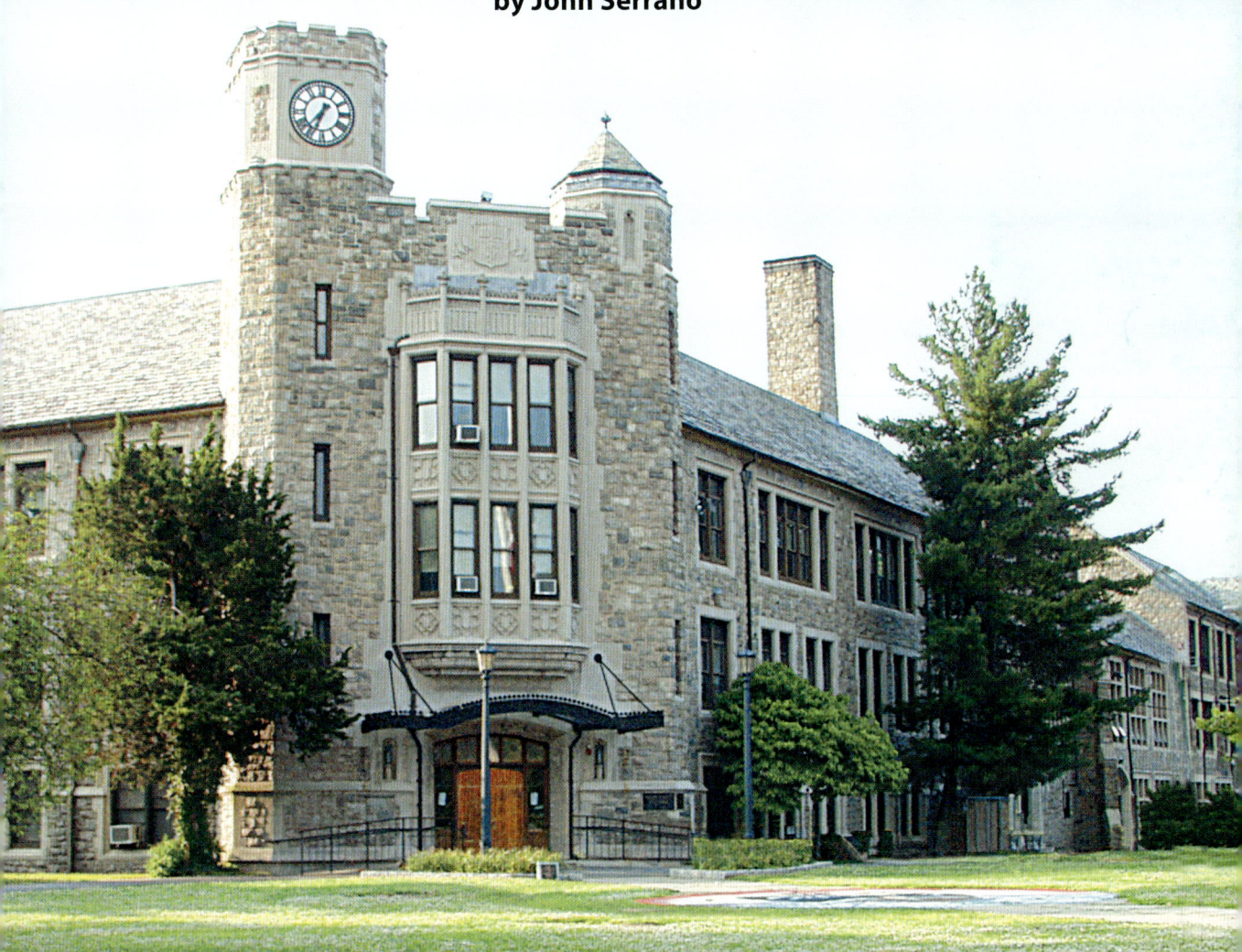

This is my old school.

This is my new school.

My old school had a small playground. We had swings and a slide.

5

My new school has a playground, too. We have swings, but no slide.

7

My old school had a small library. It had a rug to sit on. I liked to sit and read books there.

9

My new school has a big library. It has many books, and it has computers, too.

11

My old school had a lizard.
Our lizard lived in a cage.

My new school does not have a lizard. But we do have a fish! It lives in a bowl.

I had many friends at my old school.

15

I have many friends at my new school, too.